FIRST BIOGRAPHIES

Frederick Douglass

Cassie Mayer

Heinemann Library
Chicago, Illinois

Customer Service **888-454-2279**

Visit our Web site at **www.heinemannlibrary.com**

Photo research by Tracy Cummins
Designed by Kimberly R. Miracle
Maps by Mapping Specialists, Ltd.
Printed and bound in China by South China Printing Company

10 09 08 07
10 9 8 7 6 5 4 3 2 1

10 Digit ISBN: 1-4034-9974-8 (hc)   1-4034-9983-7 (pb)

Library of Congress Cataloging-in-Publication Data
Mayer, Cassie.
  Frederick Douglass / Cassie Mayer.
    p. cm. -- (First biographies)
  Includes bibliographical references and index.
  ISBN-13: 978-1-4034-9974-5 (hc)
  ISBN-13: 978-1-4034-9983-7 (pb)
  1. Douglass, Frederick, 1818-1895--Juvenile literature. 2. African American abolitionists--Biography--Juvenile literature. 3. Abolitionists--United States--Biography--Juvenile literature. 4. Antislavery movements--United States--History--19th century--Juvenile literature. I. Title.
  E449.D75M373 2008
  973.7'114092--dc22
  [B]

Acknowledgements
The author and publisher are grateful to the following for permission to reproduce copyright material: ©Corbis **pp. 5** (Bettmann), **12** (Bettmann), **14, 18** (Bettmann), **19** (Bettman), **20** (Kelly-Mooney Photography), **21** (Bettmann), **22** (Bettmann), **23** (Bettmann); ©Getty Images **pp. 6** (Hulton Archive), **11** (Hulton Archive); ©The Granger Collection **pp. 4, 10, 16**; ©Library of Congress Prints and Photographs Division **pp. 15, 17**; ©North Wind Picture Archives **pp. 7, 8, 9, 23**.

Cover image reproduced with permission of ©Corbis (Bettmann). Back cover image reproduced with permission of the ©Library of Congress Prints and Photographs Division.

Every effort has been made to contact copyright holders of any material reproduces in this book.
Any omissions will be rectified in subsequent printings if notice is given to the publisher.

Contents

Introduction

Frederick Douglass was a great leader.
A leader helps change things.

Douglass was a great speaker.
He spoke against slavery.

Slaves were people owned by other people. Douglass believed slavery was wrong.

Early Life

Douglass was born in 1818.
He lived in Maryland.

Douglass was born a slave.

Slaves could not choose how they lived.

Learning to Read and Write

Sophia Auld

Slaves were not allowed to be taught.
But a woman taught Douglass the
alphabet.

Douglass learned how to read and write.
He became a great writer.

Escape from Slavery

Douglass escaped slavery in 1838.

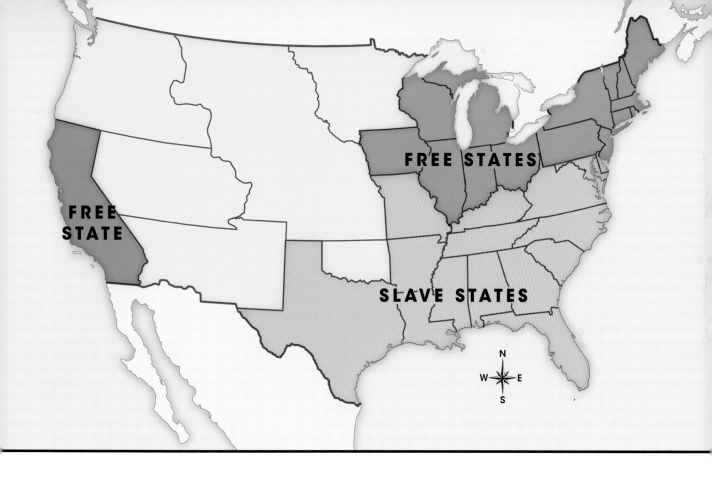

FREE STATES

FREE STATE

SLAVE STATES

N
W E
S

He escaped to the northern states.
Some northern states did not have slavery.

William Lloyd Garrison

In 1841, Douglass heard a man speak against slavery. Douglass was excited by his speech.

Speaking Out

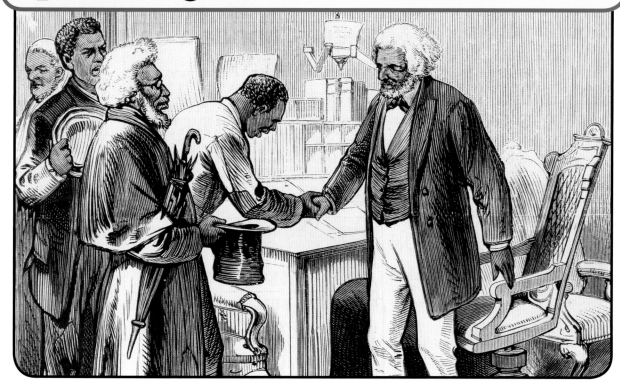

Douglass decided he should give speeches.
He became a great speaker.

Douglass spoke against slavery.
He believed all people should be free.

Working with Lincoln

Douglass worked with Abraham Lincoln.
He was a great leader.

Lincoln was president of the country.
He spoke against slavery.

Lincoln was killed in 1865. Douglass gave a speech to remember him.

Telling His Story

Douglass's desk

Douglass wrote a book in 1845.
He wrote about his life as a slave.

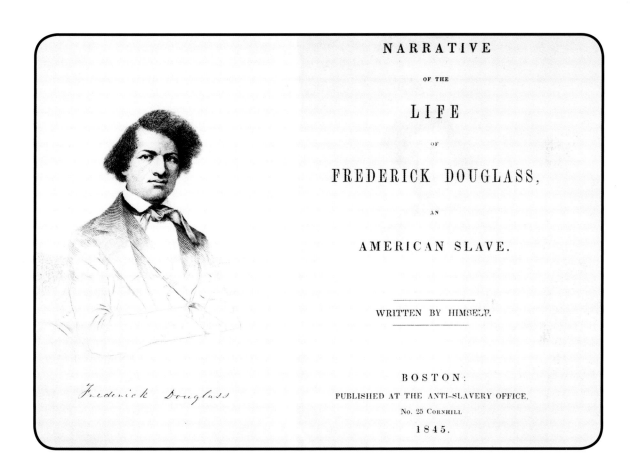

It was read by many people.
It is still read by many people.

Why We Remember Him

Frederick Douglass was a great leader. He believed all people should be free.

Picture Glossary

escape to leave secretly

slavery when people own other people

Timeline

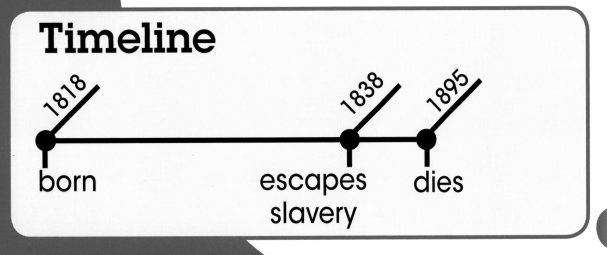

1818 — born

1838 — escapes slavery

1895 — dies

23

Index

Note to Parents and Teachers

This series introduces prominent historical figures, focusing on the significant events of each person's life and their impact on American society. Illustrations and primary sources are used to enhance students' understanding of the text.

The text has been carefully chosen with the advice of a literacy expert to enable beginning readers success while reading independently or with moderate support. An expert in the field of early childhood social studies curriculum was consulted to provide interesting and appropriate content.

You can support children's nonfiction literacy skills by helping students use the table of contents, headings, picture glossary, and index.